The Sorority Recruitment (Rush) Survival Guide

and then some.......

Table of Contents

INTRODUCTION

I chose to write this book after meetings with anxious young women (and their parents) that were going through sorority recruitment. After spending hours and hours conveying this information I was asked to write it all down. Having two daughters and some other family members go through the process, a well as going through the process myself; I have a very honest and positive view about recruitment. I am also an interview coach with years of experience coaching others for jobs, college and recruitment.

It was both exhilarating and nerve-racking guiding my own daughters through the process. As a parent, you send them off to college, but unlike high school they are not with you and most of what they do is out of your control. It is a right of passage and believe it or not the whole experience will help them in life. My oldest daughter was her sororities Vice President of Recruitment, so to say the least I am very familiar with the do's and don'ts of the recruitment process.

While being in the Greek System sometimes gets a bad rap, there are so many positives and benefits from being a member of a Greek organization. You will hear over and over sometimes jokingly, the phrase, "There is a house for everyone." The truth of the matter is this is totally an accurate statement. While the recruitment process may seem superficial and harsh to some, it strangely ends up working out for those who really want to be part of the Greek System. There are those situations in which some women realize that being in a sorority is not for them, so they decide to drop out. Those who decide to embrace it, realize that they will make life long friends and gain life experiences that are invaluable to their personal growth.

To be successful in the recruitment process, you have to approach it like interviewing for a job. If you show your best and most authentic self you will end up in a sorority where you will be comfortable. Speaking from personal experiences many of my best friends today are women who I met in my sorority.

Going through recruitment can be as, or even more scary than the first day of high school. There are so many questions, so many rules and so many things you should and should not do. I decided to write this book so that you can present your best you, so that you have the most opportunities and choices when it comes to picking a sorority to join.

If you follow my suggestions you will feel more at ease going through recruitment and it will hopefully enable you to enjoy the process and make the right choice for you. You will receive lots of advice from people, but I feel that this is the most objective realistic advice to optimize your experience.

Glossary of Terms

First let's start out with the most basic thing about the Greek System. The Greek letters that are used for each of the houses and how to pronounce them are shown below. It's really the only thing Greek about being in a sorority (except maybe wearing an occasional toga to a party-more about that later). One of the worst mistakes to make is to pronounce someone's sorority incorrectly while you are talking to them. So practice up and get the letters and their pronunciation down pat

A	B	Γ	Δ	E	Z
Alpha	Beta	Gamma	Delta	Epsilon	Zeta
(al-fah)	(bay-tah)	(gam-ah)	(del-ta)	(ep-si-lon)	(zay-tah)

H	Θ	I	K	Λ	M
Eta	Theta	Iota	Kappa	Lambda	Mu
(ay-tah)	(thay-tah)	(eye-o-tah)	(cap-pah)	(lamb-dah)	(mew)

N	Ξ	O	Π	P	Σ
Nu	Xi	Omicron	Pi	Rho	Sigma
(new)	(zie)	(om-e-cron)	(pie)	(roe)	(sig-mah)

T	Y	Φ	X	Ψ	Ω
Tau	Upsilon	Phi	Chi	Psi	Omega
(taw)	(up-si-lon)	(fie)	(kie)	(sigh)	(oh-may-gah)

Glossary of Terms (cont.)

House

Refers to the physical building that the sorority women live in. If someone is in the Greek System no one says, "What sorority are you in," they say, What house are you in? Also known as the chapter house.

Formal
Recruitment

There are various forms of recruitment and each Greek system has their own way of organizing Recruitment. Formal recruitment (usually at the beginning of the school year) is usually a set amount of days/time, during part of the year for the process. It usually lasts about a week. Prospective members sign up, submit their personal information and participate in an organized schedule set by the Panhellenic Association at the university. This can happen prior to school starting in the fall or sometime during the school year. You can find out how your University Panhellenic Association runs their formal rush on their website.

Informal Recruitment

This style of recruitment usually happens throughout the year informally. If some of the sororities do not reach their full capacity during formal recruitment they will choose to participate in informal rush. Girls can visit the houses throughout the year and some members will have women they have befriended that chose not to participate in formal rush visit to learn more about their house. Women can be asked to become new members of a house anytime after the first new member class is initiated.

Recommendation

Sometimes referred to as a RIF or "Rec." This is a letter of recommendation by an Alumna from a specific sorority. This is something that is very beneficial for every prospective member to turn in prior to recruitment to each sorority's, Vice President of Recruitment. More on this in the recommendation section of the book.

Recruitment Counselor

This is a designated sorority member of the Greek community that will help to guide you and your recruitment group through the formal recruitment process. She will usually escort you the first few days of recruitment when everyone in your group has the same schedule and houses to visit. After the first selections are made and everyone has different houses to visit they will be there through the whole process to answer questions you may have. You will not know (they should not tell you) which sorority they are affiliated with. It is imperative that they stay neutral in the process. They will be there when you get your list each day of the houses you will visit. They have usually gone through extensive training about how to handle difficult situations during the process.

House Tours

This day or days usually take place after the first round of selections, so it would be considered the second party. It is a chance for perspective members to see each house and what amenities each one has.

Sleeping Porch

This is a designated large room in the house in which there are many bunk beds and each woman that sleeps in it will have their own bed provided. They are usually 24-7 dark and quiet. Most houses have them, but some don't. Some have in-room or sleeping porch options. It's a good thing to find out during house tours.

Annex

Some houses have an additional building or adjacent building to their physical house. This is usually reserved for upper classmen, but it differs from university to university and house to house.

Hazing	_Webster defines it as follows: the action of hazing; especially : an initiation process involving harassment._ In reality most sororities are watched so closely by their national entities. Unfortunately, hazing does rarely happen, but not in the way that most people hear about. Most Panhellenic associations do not condone any behavior in which a member is "forced" to do something as a group or even on their own. For example, in most cases scavenger hunts, dressing a certain way are not even tolerated. If there is hazing any member should contact their Panhellenic or Nationals organization. Most universities and National sororities have a zero tolerance policy on hazing.
Big Sister	This is an upper classmen in the new member's sorority that they have formed a special bond with over the first few months. They usually have a mutual affection for each other. There is usually a special celebration when big and little sisters are chosen. You will have a special bond forever. Each new member is usually assigned an upper classmen immediately that will "look after" them and help them with the adjustment to college life. This is not the same thing as a big sister. Each house a different name for it. It is usually some type of "buddy."

House Mother/Director *This is a woman who lives in the chapter house. It is usual and customary for a sorority to have someone that lives in as a mother figure, and helps to manage the house. It varies in every house what their responsibilities are. They usually have an apartment in a section of the chapter house. It is not necessary for them to be an alumna of that particular sorority. The amount of responsibility she has, varies from house to house.*

Chapter Room *This is a designated room in the sorority that only initiated members may enter.*

Chapter Meeting *This is a mandatory meeting that new and active members will attend each week. Before the new members are initiated the chapter meetings will start in another room of the house and will continue in the chapter room without the new members. This is where they find out most information about what is going on at the house each week.*

House Bill/Dues *This is a quarterly/semester bill that you will receive for your room and board. Payment is usually due around the same time that your tuition is due.*

| Room Draw | *This is the process for choosing which room you will have each quarter if you live in. Usually when living in you will change rooms each quarter/semester. By participating in sorority activities you will acquire points. Those with the most points get to choose their rooms first and so on. For people not living in a chapter house this does not apply.* |

| Social Member | *Some sororities allow members to live out and pay for only the social aspects of the house.* |

| Alumni | *This is a member who has remained active in the house throughout their years in college and graduated as a member of their sorority. If you drop your house at any time during college you may not consider yourself an alumna of that organization.* |

| Initiation | *This is the ceremony in which new members become active members. There are many traditions that every house follows. There are requirements that new members must have to be able to be initiated. They must have a certain GPA, have lived up to the standards of the house, and have learned the history of the house. They are usually required to pass a small test on the history of the organization and its founders. It is a very special time in a new member's experience.* |

Formals	*This is a sorority or fraternity dance in which they extend or are extended an invitation for their formal dance. There are usually a few each year for each house. They tend to be about as dressy as a high school homecoming dance.*
Greek Row	*This is usually the main street in a Greek system. It differs from every school. It tends to be the street where most things happen in the Greek System. It is often the street where the first houses where established historically.*
Greek Week	*This is a designated week during the year in which sororities and fraternities have games, philanthropic fundraisers and fun activities for a week. It is a friendly competition.*
Study Room	*This is a designated space in a chapter house where there are surroundings for studying and usually are 24 quiet. This is only the case for members who live in chapter houses.*
Sister	*This is a term that each member refers to the other members in her sorority. It is a true statement in that the minute you become a member you are considered a member of the family.*

Legacy	*A legacy is a family member who was an active member in a certain sorority. It usually refers to Grandmother, Mother or Sister. It can have different advantages at every house. It depends on their policy on how they choose to deal with legacy situations. There will be spaces to provide legacy information on your recruitment form.*
Dirty Rushing	*This is something that goes against the strict rules laid out by the Panhellenic Association of each University. If a prospective new member reports any of this happening, then the house can be fined and put on probation. Some examples of this may be, but are not limited to:*

- *Trying to contact the prospective new member outside of rush hours by texting or communicating. This is strictly forbidden.*
- *There may not be more than one girl talking to a prospective member for an extended period of time during recruitment at one time.*
- *They may not talk about other houses to the prospective member during recruitment.*
- *They may not ask if you have any sisters, mothers, grandmothers (legacies) in other houses.*
- *They should not be speaking negatively about other houses.*

- *They may not give you anything to take with you at any time during recruitment.*

There are other forms of dirty rushing, but these are some of the most egregious examples. If a prospective member experiences any of this, they should report it to their Recruitment Counselor immediately.

THERE IS A HOUSE FOR EVERYONE

When you consider that most schools have many sororities, most having very different women as members there is truly a house for every girl. It is very similar when you are making the decision as to what college you will attend based on certain criteria. The same situation holds true when you are choosing which house you will join through formal or informal recruitment. The worst mistake you can make is to have a preconceived notion about which house you would like to be a member of before recruitment starts. Many times the information that you may be basing this decision on is inaccurate. The most important thing that you should do is come to your own conclusions, based on your personal experiences through the recruitment process. If you consider that every year there are new members coming in and graduating, some of the things you may have heard both positive and negative may not be true.

It is important that you do not let others influence your choices. This is probably most challenging when it is a legacy situation. It is a special situation when grandmothers, mothers, daughters and sisters have their sorority in common. It is just as important that you feel comfortable where you will be spending a majority of time during college. It is also important, that you do not listen to others going through the recruitment process at the same time as you. Emotions are running high and while it may seem like the people going through recruitment with you are trying to be helpful it is important to remember it is a competitive situation. Rely on your own intuition and feelings through the process. Go with your gut.

As you go through the process give every house a chance. You may meet someone one day you are not that fond of, but after the next visit you may meet others you really click with.

If you consider that most houses have many members, it is likely that not every one of them will be your best friend. It is true, however, that most of the time many girls in your house will have your back, but you will probably find a group of women who you spend most of your time with. Very similar to high school (not the everyone having your back part). Try to have a positive outlook through the process with everyone that you meet.

RECOMMENDATIONS AND PERSONAL INFORMATION

Recommendations are an important aspect of the recruitment process. They are a letter and other pertinent information that you will have sent to each sorority's Vice President of Recruitment over the summer. This will give you an upper hand through the process. It is an advantage that a previous member has taken the time out to endorse you as a prospective member. However, it is best to find an alumna who knows you well. It is better to have an acquaintance that you may not know well, but will vouch for you than not having any recommendation at all. You can find people through family or friend referrals. Many people put a plea on social messaging asking for help from their friends. Most alumni are happy to help if they know someone in your family. Some houses require that you have one. Most are sent in a month prior to formal rush. It can be someone from any chapter for a particular house. It does not have to be from the exact university in which you are attending.

Personal Information Checklist

You will need one copy for each house that you have someone send a recommendation to. Preferably every house.

- Resume
- Attractive picture (usually a senior picture, wallet size or 3X5 headshot picture)
- Recommendation Form (RIF form)
- Letter to Alumna writing recommendation for you.
- Pre-stamped envelope to each sorority VP of Recruitment
- Copy of RIF form if you can access it.

Resume

This should be a one page information sheet about you. It should have your name, address, cell phone and email address. You should have your high school at the top under education. Your GPA should be listed if it is over 3.3. You should put your weighted and un-weighted GPA. If you have a high class rank you can put that as well (top 10%).

Then list your work experience. If you do not have a lot of work experience put your experiences in high school as you would list your work experience. For example if you were very involved in sports put which team you were on and all the experiences or awards you gained during that experience.

They are looking for activities and leadership on your resume. List everything you were involved with in high school. Things to stay away from are things having to do with religion or politics, just as you would in a job interview.

You should have an activities and awards section on your resume as well. Here you will list extra curricular activities and awards such as Team Captain, Most Inspirational, etc...

It is also great to have a service section of your resume as sororities are very involved in philanthropic causes and they look very favorably on service.

Lastly, you can add an interests section which is your hobbies that you like to do in your spare time.

Just as if you were applying for a job, houses are looking for women that have had previous experiences that may help them in Greek Life. For example, if they were Treasurer of their Student Body they may think, "Great, she can be our Treasurer!" If a prospective member has a high GPA, it is a positive because grades are very important to each house. They will use your past to try to gage if you will be successful in the future. Therefore, your resume is their first glimpse into what you have done before you start the recruitment process.

PERSONAL PICTURE THAT ACCOMPANIES RECOMMENDATION

This should be a head shot or it can be a full body shot if it is not with any props. If it is a full body picture, it should not be a shot where you are laying in a field of flowers, just simple. The best choice is a head shot. Usually people use their senior picture. Only send one picture with each recommendation. Some people go way overboard and send in a whole scrapbook. This is not good. Keep it simple. They are getting hundreds of recommendations, so you can imagine the amount of information they have to go through. You will provide the person writing your recommendation with a picture to send in. Write your name on the back of the picture in case it gets separated from your resume and Recommendation form.

Example of head shot that is appropriate

RECOMMENDATION FORM/RIF FORM

This is a form that the alumna from a particular house will fill out and send in with her recommendation. You can go on the national web-sites of a lot of the houses to download a PDF of the form that you can send to the person writing your recommendation. You want to make it as easy as possible for them to write the recommendation. Some sororities will not allow access to a person who is not a member into their web-site. The person writing the recommendation will be able to access this form themselves as an alumna on each web-site. Take time to read some of the recommendation forms so that you have an idea about what type of information they will have to provide about you. If it is someone that does not know you well, you can make sure they have all the pertinent information that they will need. They will also be writing a recommendation letter to accompany the RIF form and resume. If it is someone that knows you, it should not be a problem. If it is someone that does not know you then they will be looking at your resume for information to put into their letter.

LETTER TO ALUMNI

This should be a cover letter that you write to each person writing a recommendation for you. Thank them in advance for helping you and give them information that you would like highlighted in your Rec. You can add a small gift card for their time if you would like.

PRE-STAMPED/ADDRESSED ENVELOPE

Along with the picture, resume and RIF form you need to include a pre-stamped, addressed envelope. It should be addressed to the person that is in charge of recruitment for that sorority. You will be able to find this information on each University's Panhellenic web-site or on the site of that particular sorority at your university. They will have the information under recruitment. Make sure that it is updated information for the time frame you are participating in recruitment. This position changes yearly, and some houses are better at updating their sites than others. Again, your goal is to make it as easy for the person writing the recommendation as possible to be able to send it in to the correct person. The national sites for each sorority are usually pretty good at updating their information, so that is also another option to find out who the current VP of Recruitment is.

You should be starting this process to find people for recommendations shortly after you figure out where you will be attending college, or during the early summer at the latest. The worst thing you can do is leave it until the last minute. Then you are not giving the person writing your recommendations enough time to turn it in. It is also appropriate to ask them to let you know when they send it in, so that you can send them a gentle reminder to do so. Many times the information lands on someone's desk in a pile and they forget to do it. That is the main rationale behind making it as easy as possible for them. A great way to send a reminder is to send them a thank you note beyond what you said in your letter to them. This is a note where you can thank them again for their kindness in supporting you for their sorority.

Recommendations are a step that many people do not know about, or ignore. The goal is to increase your options and odds for having a successful recruitment. This is the first step that is completely in your control to make that happen.

Formal Recruitment
&
General Do's and Don'ts

Formal recruitment is probably the most recognized process when people refer to Recruitment or Rush. This is an organized, scheduled and very strict process that is set forth by each university's Panhellenic Association. The chapter houses have very strict rules that they must follow or face severe fines and possible probation. Formal Recruitment is usually about 5-7 days depending on how many sororities there are on a particular campus. The more houses the longer the process takes to get through.

The major thing to keep in mind is that most of the women are just as nervous as you are and they can empathize with you as they went through the same process. Their goal is to find the women that they feel will fulfill the ideals and goals of each house. These can be very different from house to house and it is the prospective member's job to ask questions to figure out if they match up with their desires for their living situation and college housing experience.

The running theme that you will find throughout all of this information is that if you can make it easier for everyone involved you will have a better experience. How this pertains to Formal Recruitment is that you need to be prepared before you go into this process. Referring back to a job interview, you need to be prepared to talk about experiences that you have had that tell them about who you are and what you have to offer. You also need to have great questions that you can ask them, so there are no awkward moments or pauses.

So here is your homework and again, do this far enough in advance so that you can give it good thought and practice. It may sound strange, but this too will increase your odds of success.

Homework:

Practice your handshake. It should be very firm and I say very because many women have a limp handshake and this is a huge turn off. A major reason people do not get jobs is because of wimpy handshake and the same goes for recruitment. No one likes a limp, clammy handshake and it does not make a great first impression. When you shake someone's hand you should look them directly in the eye and shake their hand firmly. If they don't put theirs out to shake stick yours out with authority and say, "Hi, I am Laurie!" It is also a good idea to subtlety wipe your hand off right before the girls come out to greet you. Every time a new member (someone you have not met before) comes up to meet you, they should be greeted with a handshake and great eye contact. This is so important and often overlooked! This holds true for your entire life, not just recruitment.

Think about some questions that may come up and how you will answer them. Do not just give one word answers. Try to say something interesting within each answer. Remember, you are trying to make it easy for the person talking to you, so she has a positive experience with you. If you can come up with something that makes you stand out, that is unusual or unique that is the best case scenario. If you think about it from their perspective, they are meeting hundreds of girls and when it comes time to reflect on who they liked during the day, the women that had that certain, unique thing will stick out in their mind. This can be a positive or negative thing, so keep that in mind. It can work for or against you. If you say or do something that is not flattering they will remember that as well. Again, this is something totally in your control, so take advantage of it and make sure you are positive.

Here are two examples:

My daughter, had an internship with Cosmopolitan Magazine in New York during high school. She had that on her resume and talked about it during recruitment. As the recruitment process went on when girls would come up and talk with her, they said, "Oh, you are the Cosmo Girl." They all thought it was such a cool experience and it was a great unusual talking point.

Now let's look at something that could have been a disaster during recruitment. This is an example of turning a negative into a positive. My younger daughter, lost her voice two days into recruitment. We discussed it and I advised her to take the bull by the horns and turn it into something funny. I said that they will remember you as the girl with the funny voice or the girl who lost her voice, but was so cool and positive about it. When she introduced herself, she said, "Hi, sorry if I sound like an 8th grade boy going through puberty." Everyone always laughed and it broke the ice immediately. You must remember that you will have such a limited time with each person that everything is exaggerated (both positively and negatively). They were once in your position, so they have empathy for you.

It is important to be enthusiastic and positive. It's just as if you were in a play and you had to exaggerate your feelings to your audience because you want to build a rapport quickly.

Here are some questions that you can think about ahead of time to better prepare yourself and increase your odds of success:

<u>Where are you from</u>? Most people would give a one word answer of either their city or state. Now remember your job is to make it easy for them. If they have to think of fewer questions to ask you or do less talking that is what they prefer. The answer to this question is dependent on where you live (far or close from where you are attending college).

If you live far away from where you are going, you can say where you are from, how much you enjoyed growing up there, and how excited you are to go away and have lots of new experiences and meet new people. They probably will not ask you what high school you went to because they won't know about the high school unless they are familiar with where you lived. If they have never been there, you can go into detail about some great things about where you lived.

The next question will most likely be, "<u>Why did you choose to come to X University</u>."
Trust me when I say, there are those who will say, something like, "It's the only one I got into. Or, I don't know it looked good on paper." These are negative responses that actually belittle the person that you are talking to without realizing it. This is your chance to talk about how excited you are about going to such a great college. People attending a college are usually the biggest fans, so when you talk about that, it gets them excited too.

Even if you don't have a good reason for choosing your college, then you need to come up with some satisfactory reasons to discuss. It may be that your parents went there, that you love their football team, that is had the best school in which you are studying in, etc...So let's say you mention they have a great football team. You can then naturally go into asking her what it's like to go to the football games, etc.. if you prepare you can control the conversation and never have that awkward silence. You will be a breath of fresh air for sure. The conversation can go on and on if you are prepared.

The other scenario is if you live close to the college you are attending. This can be a positive or a negative. There will probably be women in the house that know you already, so there may be some good or unfavorable preconceived notions about you before recruitment starts. This is one of those situations in life that you hope that you didn't burn any bridges and did your best to be kind to others. Let's be honest here. If you were a mean girl in high school or didn't treat others well, you may have a tougher time going through recruitment. In college people learn that people change a lot from high school to college, so all is not lost. If you live close, your first question about where you are from, will probably followed up by, "Oh, where did you go to high school." The worst thing you can do at this point is start to name drop or ask her if she knows someone there or at her high school. You do not want to be considered or judged based on other people's perception of who you are talking about. Keep the conversation about you. If a member knows you from high school, she will seek you out to say hi. If the member asks you if you know a certain individual or individuals you need to keep a smile on your face and remain positive about everyone. If you knew them well and were friends it is alright to say yes, she was great and we were good friends. If you didn't know them well you can say, "I didn't know her well, but she always seemed so great." If it was someone you were not fond of, then you can say that you didn't know them, but you knew of them. You can personally use this as you are making your decision about a house. Remember that people do change; you should not make any quick decisions based on how someone was in high school.

Your next question will also most likely be, why did you choose to come to X University? You can talk about home town pride, and how much you love the area and always wanting to go there. Positive, positive, positive.

"What do you want to major in?" will most likely be another question you will be asked. Most of you have no idea what you want to major in at this point and all you are worried about right now is how recruitment is going. This is totally normal at this point, but not very interesting to talk about. Your major will probably change a few times during your college experience, so this answer will change as you journey through your education. This is an easy question for those of you who know you want to be a Doctor, Lawyer, Accountant,

Computer Science major, Teacher...etc...You can go on and on about what you want to major in and why. For those of you who have no idea, it is alright to say I am not exactly sure, but I am interested in X and Y (be thinking of some things to say) and I am looking forward to taking classes in both to see if it is something I want to pursue. Then you ask them immediately what they are majoring in, how they like it and you can elaborate by asking them about how easy or hard it is to get into classes they like, and so on.

"<u>What did you do this summer</u>?" Obviously the worst thing you can say is not that much. What could anyone say to that answer? This is the kind of thing that leads to the awkward pause.

At a minimum you were getting ready for college. You can elaborate on your job if you worked, talk about trips you may have taken, spent time with your family, or hobbies and interests you have.

Use this as a way to show what types of things you like to do and how it can relate to the sorority. You can then finish with, "What about you, what did you do this summer?" Let's say that you or the person you are talking to traveled to somewhere interesting, out of the country. This is a great time to ask if they know anything about the study abroad program at the university.
You should always try to be one question ahead.

"What do you like to do in your spare time?"
This is a great chance to talk about activities you did in high school, service projects you have participated in, etc...Again, the worst thing to say is I don't know watch TV or just chill. You would be surprised what people say. If you were passionate about something in high school, this is your chance to talk about it.

If at anytime you experience, *Dirty Rushing,* which is explained in the glossary of terms then you need to report it immediately and seriously consider if you want to be associated with a group of women that would do this. You are not supposed to be asked about anything regarding, Race, Religion, Sexual Orientation, Family Wealth, or anything else that can be interpreted as offensive or discriminatory. If someone at one house starts telling you things about another house, this is also a huge red flag. You should know that houses should be able to stand on their own without spreading rumors (which are usually unfounded) about other houses. This is a big no, no.

Along those lines, you should not be asking about anything at all having to do with any of these topics. Other topics that should not come up are: Parties, fraternities, drinking, any material items such as cars, clothing, and houses. This may seem obvious to some, but believe me it does happen.
If someone asks you what houses you have liked (Dirty Rushing) the proper response is that you have found something great at all the houses and everyone has been so nice. The

problem is that if someone tries to dirty rush you, then you should not call them out on it directly, and you should answer in a way that doesn't get you in a sticky situation as I illustrated above. If it happens you can use this as a deciding factor in which house you choose to be in.

Remember, you can say the same thing over and over again at each house. As you are preparing you can have a certain amount of questions and answers that you go over in your head and practice with someone close to you, so you will feel confident and prepared during recruitment.

<u>Major Don'ts</u>
- Do not chew gum. If you want to chew it in between houses that is fine, but make sure you get rid of it far before you get to the house.
- Do not wear 4 inch heels! You will be walking a lot and up and down stairs.
- Do not wear a tight short dress/skirt that you will be pulling on all day. Many times you will be sitting on the floor, so whatever you wear has to be comfortable and cute.
- Do not wear sequins at any point! This is not a prom, it is recruitment.
- Do not have too revealing of a top. Sometimes I see girls walking through recruitment that have more cleavage showing than they have covered. Not good.
- Do not spray tan the day before recruitment. If you feel the need to do

it, then give it a few days before in case there are any unforeseen problems that arise.

The worst thing is that you show up looking like an Oompa Loompa.

- Do not break in a new pair of shoes for recruitment. Your feet will be very sore. This won't help. If you get new shoes break them in weeks before.
- Do not be late. Get to the next house early instead of talking between and waiting until the last minute. They are on a very tight schedule and it is very unfortunate if you are late.
- Do not talk to men in front of the houses you are waiting to go into. Houses have windows and it's a good chance they are looking out waiting for you to arrive. Be on alert and your best behavior as soon as you get there.
- Do not talk about other houses or fraternities.
- Do not talk about being a legacy anywhere.
- Do not talk about what you liked or didn't like about a certain house to anyone.
- Do not tell anyone who your top choices are. Just say I would like to keep that to myself.
- Do not go out at night and obviously no drinking at any time during recruitment.
- Do not take notes on a pad of paper about houses or people you meet. If you loose it or someone finds it. not good.

- Do not wear perfume. There are so many girls in a house at once and a lot of different fragrances can be overbearing.

Do's

- Bring a light pair of flip flops in your purse, so as soon as you leave one house you can change into them to walk. Change back into your shoes right before you get to the next house.
- Bring band-aids, ibuprophen, feminine hygiene products, gel inserts in your shoes, mints/toothpaste, tissues, tide to go pen, deodorant and a water bottle to put in your purse. Small umbrella is also good to have it rain is in the forecast.
- If you feel yourself getting very nervous, ask to go to the bathroom to gather yourself together.
- Smile as much as you can.
- If you feel like you are getting dry mouth you can put a little Vaseline under your top gums. It will prevent this from happening.
- Stay hydrated-drink water, not punch. If you spill it on yourself, you will be stressed the whole day.
- Take notes on your phone as you are walking between houses (as long as it has a pass code to get in) about each house or certain girls you meet.

- Treat every house like they are your favorite house. Your goal is to have as many houses ask you back everyday to increase your options.

Days One and Two

Days one and two are usually the same type of parties, but they split up the houses because it is impossible to see all the houses in one day. So you have two days of the same thing, but at different houses. You will be assigned a Recruitment Counselor (RC) that will guide you and your group to each house. This person will stay your RC for the entire recruitment process. You will not know what sorority the person is in, so that they can remain objective. They have been trained to handle various different situations and are there to help. They will only guide you around on the first two days because after that everyone will have different schedules. They do usually meet you in the morning to make sure all is well and hand out your list for that day.

These are usually the most casual days. Some University's will provide t-shirts for these two days, so that everyone is wearing the same thing. There is usually a "what to wear" guide on the Panhellenic web-site of your university. They tend to downplay the dress code, so if you are in doubt go a little dressier.

This is your chance to make a big first impression the first day. The parties are usually very quick, so your enthusiasm level needs to be high. Practice the questions we outlined above, firm handshakes and a smile and you will be great. After the second day and you have had the chance to see each house, you will then go to the designated area and write down the houses you liked in preferential order. Remember do not discuss this with anyone. Write down every house-fill every space. The houses will then put the women they have met in preferential order and the computer will match everything up. The next morning/afternoon, you will receive a list that is now half of what your original list was for the 3rd day of recruitment. There is a chance you may have less houses than you put down. This means that you did not match up with enough houses. Don't despair, go to the houses on your list and keep an open mind. Remember, there is a house for everyone.

What is appropriate to wear: Jeans or Jean shorts if it is very hot, but not too short. No ripped jeans, please do not wear jeans that are too tight or a short jean skirt. Remember you will be sitting down. Muffin tops are not attractive and believe me no one wants to see your underwear or even worse your crack. A casual top that is cute and shows your personality. Nothing see through or too revealing. Cute, comfortable flats or sandals are appropriate. You can literally wear the same thing two days in a row (because you will be going to different houses) if you would like, but most people bring a few shirts in case something gets stained or wrinkled. Your hair and make up should be cute, but casual. No prom hairdos.

HOUSE TOURS

The third and possibly fourth day of recruitment is usually when you will tour the houses. Remember, you have to find your way around without the assistance from your RC, so don't dawdle after each party. It's helpful to put a map of the Greek System in your purse in case you forget where the houses are. You should also familiarize yourself with the Greek System before recruitment starts by driving or walking around to see where each house is.

Get to the next house on your list each time and relax if you have extra time. Each day becomes more and more dressy. This day you would wear something that they usually will categorize as business casual. This is the toughest day, because most people do not know what to make of this style of dress as there are many interpretations of this. On this day, the best thing to wear is a pair of nice dress pants with a cute blouse or top and some cute shoes. Not too high as you will be going up and down a lot of stairs, but not sandals. You can also wear a skirt and a cute top as well. No jean skirts or jeans on these days. Keep in mind that you are touring houses and need to be comfortable walking up and down stairs. While you are touring their house, try to keep the conversation going by asking them questions about the house. Do they sleep in their rooms or in a sleeping porch? Where do they study? Ask about their meals and if they have out of state lockers if you are in that situation. You will be meeting new girls today and you will probably see girls from your first visit as well. Try and remember their names if you can. After you have gone to all your houses for the second visit (one or two days depending on how it is run) you will then go back to the designated area to put your remaining houses in preferential order. The houses will do the same and the amount of houses you have left is again, cut in half. This is probably the hardest day because houses are really starting to narrow down their choices. Once again, don't despair if you do not get your top choices. Keep and open mind and continue on.

THEME OR PHILANTHROPY DAY

The next day or 5th day is usually a themed day. Possibly a day in which all the houses talk about their philanthropies. Service is a very important part of life in the Greek System. Each house traditionally has a philanthropy they spend the year raising funds for hosting different events. If they have this day, they will usually spend time telling you about what they do for this cause and you can possibly participate in a task to help that cause out. The dress for this day will be something you may wear to a nice brunch, or daytime wedding. I would say a cotton or casual dress and some type of heeled shoe, dressy flat, but not flat sandals. The parties are longer now and you will be seeing girls you have met before coming back to talk to you again. You should be getting to know a lot more about the house and its members. At this point and you should start to have stronger feelings about where you belong. After this party you will narrow the houses down to around 3 or 4 houses in preferential order for your final day (Preference Day). The houses will do the same and the next day you will have your top 3 or 4 houses left to visit.

Preference Day

Preference Day. This is usually the dressiest day. This IS NOT prom. A dressy, short (not too short) dress is appropriate. Something you may have worn to a Homecoming dance in high school. No sequins. I have seen dresses that are full length and look more like wedding dresses than a dress appropriate for recruitment. No long dresses, no prom hairdos, and no 5 inch heels. This is your last chance to make a good impression. The houses will choose different types of themes they would like to have for this day. Some will choose to be reflective and sentimental and some will choose to be spirited. You can get a good feeling about a house on this day. Pay attention to where you feel comfortable. You will usually have one girl who you have seen a few times, and possibly formed a bond with spend the whole time with you. They cannot ask you which house you want to live in and you should not tell them. You will be able to tell and so will they. The most important thing is that you look at the other women that are visiting that house as well with you. This will be the women you will be spending the next 3-4 years with. This is an important thing that is overlooked. The prospective new members are so busy trying to meet the girls in the house that they forget to look around and see who their peers are at that moment. This day can be emotional for many girls, but not everyone. There is no right way or wrong way to feel. Just pay attention to your intuition and your heart and it will lead you to the right place. That may sound very corny, however it is true. Listen to your intuition.

After you visit all the remaining houses you will then go to the designated place and put the houses you visited during Preference Day in preferential order. Take your time to think about the previous week. Where have you felt the most comfortable? Were there any red flags? What did I like or dislike about any of them? Take your time. Do not talk to anyone. I cannot stress this enough. I know people who had their mind made up, spoke to someone and it changed their mind and they did not end up happy. This is a decision that you need to make on your own. You will be around and possibly living with these women for the next four years. These will be your friends for many years to come. When I got married, two of my sorority sisters were in my wedding and we are still close friends today!

Bid Day

This is the day you have been waiting for. Early the next morning after you have put your houses in preferential order, everyone gathers at the same place and you receive your Bid card/invitation to join one of the houses you have been visiting all week. You will open the card and then gather with everyone who will be part of your new member class. Members from the house will usually come down to meet you to take you all back to the chapter house to see all your new sisters. There is usually a huge celebration at all the houses, with lots of pictures, music and screaming. In most cases, everyone is where they should be in. Some are disappointed if they did not get an invitation to a house they thought they would end up in, however so many times they end up happy as ever, together with their new family. There truly is a house for everyone. Many universities will guarantee a house for everyone going through recruitment. This is a question you can usually find the answer to on the University Panhellenic website.

Informal Recruitment

Informal Recruitment usually happens in the winter or spring if a sorority needs to obtain more members for budgeting purposes. Some universities do not have formal recruitment (usually smaller Greek systems) and solely rely on informal recruitment. Many times incoming students do not know they want to go through the recruitment process upon entering a new University. After some investigation they learn about the Greek System and realize it is something they would like to participate in. They can choose to go through Informal Rush.

Girls that are not in houses may make friends with girls who are in a house. They may decide that this is something they want to learn more about. They may also choose to go through informal recruitment instead of waiting a whole year for the next formal recruitment process. Another situation that may take place is that if someone transfers from another university and wants to go through recruitment they can choose the informal route as well. It is very casual and there are usually no organized days like there are in formal recruitment. There may be open houses, or dinners in which informal recruits are invited to come over and meet some of the members. Houses will decide to invite the prospective new member to join or decide that they are not the right fit. Formal recruitment, although it may seem harder is a generally a better way to go if you can. It enables you to bond together at the same time with the new member class. New informal members are welcomed in with open arms, but it is somewhat like coming into a new high school after school has already started.

What You Should Look For?

This is probably the most important aspect of recruitment. Everyone is always very concerned about the people that they meet during the recruitment process at every chapter. While this is very important one often overlooked aspect is who is visiting the house at the same time that you are. Look around at the other women during each day of recruitment. This becomes more important as the week goes on. These are the women that will be in your new member class. These are the women that will be your closest friends during your time at the sorority and most likely for the rest of your life. You can get a sense of who they are and make an opinion if you think these are women you can see yourself living with. Find out what year in school most of the people who are recruiting you are. If you see that most of the people you like are seniors, keep in mind they will be graduating. It is important that you meet the lower classmen as these will be the leaders of the house and the women you get to know during your time at the sorority. Some chapters even bring in women from other chapters to help out, so it is important to ask questions such as, what they like about the university and sorority. You will get an idea if they are going to your school or not.

While a beautiful chapter house is wonderful to live in, it is very important that you do not choose a house based on what it looks like or what the bathroom is like. The most important thing is the women that live there. Most sororities keep their houses up and this is usually not an issue. Also know that during recruitment the houses are looking their best and generally do not stay that immaculate during the year. There are some houses that rent furniture and empty the closets in the rooms so that they appear larger, so be careful not to judge based on these things. It is not appropriate to ask about this during recruitment, but keep in mind that it does happen. You can ask about the food and if you have dietary restrictions you can ask if they make accommodations for various things like vegetarians, peanut allergies, etc. Another aspect that is often overlooked is the location of the house. Find out where most of the activities happen in the Greek System. There is usually one street where a lot of the activity is. Some girls choose to live closer to this street, but there are those who choose to live away from the high level of activity. It is something to look at whatever your preference may be.

Other things that are appropriate to ask about and that you may want to look for are: How many of the girls that are in-state versus out of state? A lot of people who are in-state go home during the weekend. If you are out of state, it is nice to know there are women that will be around over the weekends. Usually in-state women are great about bringing the out of state women home if they go. The women really do look after each other. If you have a car, you can ask if there is parking available or what most people do. It is recommended that most freshmen do not have a car at school for many reasons. I agree with this. Cars come with a lot of responsibility and costs and add a lot of stress to freshmen year.

I am sure that you are seeing a pattern with what I am advising. The most important thing is to go with your gut and intuition. You will get a feeling from the house and the women in it. You should feel comfortable and a bond with them by the end of the week. If you only have a bond with one person you meet, you may want to ask yourself further questions before you decide. Try to meet as many people as you can to get an idea about the culture and feel of the house.

What They Are Looking For?

Just as you will be looking at them, they will be seeing if you are someone they can see fitting in to their house. They are looking for well rounded, intelligent, personable, and friendly women who look like they are embracing the process and have a strong desire to be in the Greek System.

Remember that they have your resume and recruitment form that you have filled out prior to the start of recruitment. GPA is extremely important in the Greek System. Houses are rated by the Panhellenic Council every quarter to see who has the highest grades. They look for new members who have a strong GPA and this will definitely help in the process. It is much like the college application process. They are looking for individuals who have extra curricular activities and have had leadership and service in high school. Most of these things are a very important part of Greek Life, so they will see that if you have done this in the past you will most likely participate in these things throughout your time at the house. If you have leadership experience, many times these women end up being the leaders in the house, so this is also a bonus. Sports, clubs, theatre, dance, cheer are also a plus because all these skills you will use.

Looking put together is also an important aspect of recruitment. While a common misconception is that every person in the Greek System has to be gorgeous it just simply is not true. It is important that you do present yourself in the best possible way. If it looks like you are taking the process seriously and are trying to put your best self forward they will appreciate that. If it looks like you rolled out of bed, and are not taking the process seriously, that will probably be noted as well.

Move In Day

In some situations you may be able to move directly into the chapter house when recruitment ends. You may live in a dorm your first year and then be able to move in sophomore year. Either way this applies to both. First of all, if you are a freshman that gets to move in right away this can be a crazy time as all the new members are moving in at once. The members will be there to help you. The biggest mistake people make is to bring too much "stuff." Do not bring a ton of picture frames with pictures of your high school friends. Bring a few empty frames as you will have new pictures with your new sisters very quickly to display. It's also great to bring a few family pictures. You will want to scope out the room you will be living in to see what you will need before buying everything. It is fun to decorate your room, so while it is fun to have a theme some of those items can be purchased after you move in. The essentials you should have ready to go are:

- Bedding-twin size flat and fitted sheets, pillow and pillow case. Do not bring a ton of throw pillows. Some people like a mattress pad or a foam top. Costco has a great one at a great price. Duvets are best as they are easier to wash then washing the whole comforter. Depending on how warm it is where you go, a blanket may be desirable, but just a down comforter and duvet is best. It makes it easier to make the bed.

- Thin, velvet hangers. These are the best invention. You can get so many more hangers in the closets which is important as space is usually very limited. You can get these at Costco or Target in boxes of 35-50.

- Shower caddy: Not too big. It must have holes in it so that the water can drain out. Do not get Costco sized shampoo, conditioner; etc...as it is hard to fit everything in the caddy and it becomes very heavy.

The best thing to do is buy your caddy when you are getting your toiletries so you can put them all in it to see if they will fit.

- Velcro Towel cover up to wrap around you to walk to and from the shower.

- 3M hooks, various sizes. These will be the best way to hang everything from your hair dryer to pictures on the wall. Most sororities and dorms discourage using nails, so these are a life saver.

- Power strips and extension cords-bring two extension cords and a power strip.

- Canvas Clothes hamper that has a removable mesh bag. They have a great one that is at Target. The removable bag makes it easy to take your clothes to the laundry room.

- Plastic Rubbermaid hooks that go over the closet or room door. You will use these for towels, coats, purses, etc.

- Combination lock-used for closet door, a drawer or out of state locker. Always good to have something that has a lock on it.

- If you are in a hotter climate you may want a fan that clips on the bed.

- Computer printer (not too big with wireless capacity) printer paper.

- Clothes. Don't bring all your clothes to start unless you live out of state this may not be avoided. One of the best things about being in a sorority is that you will have many new sisters that are usually more than willing to share clothes. You will be buying new sweatshirts, and t-shirts, so do not bring a lot of things with your high school on them. You will need a few nice dresses early on so make sure to bring shoes and some dresses. Slippers to wear around the house and flip flops for the shower are important.

- 2 towels. Do not bring more than two towels. Space is limited.

- Toiletries, hair dryers, and other personal hygiene items.

  Things to wait until you move in but are essential:

- Bulletin Board-wait to see where you are living so you can get the correct size.

- Desk lamp-again you may want a floor lamp or desk lamp. Wait and see what fits best.

- Plastic drawers. The container store has the best ones. They have multi colored drawers and can fit next to your bed, desk or sometimes in your closet. These are great, but what to see what size will fit.
- Rug if needed-wait to see what fits.
- A few little glass canisters for items that will go on your desk. Wait to see how big your desk or dressing area is.
- Usually desks, chairs and dressers are provided.
- Curtains, if it is allowed. Wait to see what size you will need.

Saying Goodbye

If you are taking your daughter to school and helping her move in, this is the hardest part for parents. After you help her get moved in, it is important for you to let her go so she can get to know her new sisters/roommates. The first few days are very important when someone is moving into a sorority/dorm. This is when initial friendships and bonds happen and it is very important that parents are not around. If you live close, it is important to encourage your daughter to stay at the house/dorm and not come home in the beginning. They will miss out on many things and getting to know the new member class. They are all in the same situation and they will have each other to lean on. You have prepared them their whole life for this moment. Be proud and let them spread their wings.

Friends for Life

If you ask most people that were in the Greek System they will say that the people they stay in contact with are those who they met while in their house. I can say that my closest friends today, are from my sorority. Having moved around the country it was always great to meet someone from my sorority. As you have an immediate bond and something to talk about. The upperclassmen view the new members as their sisters immediately and will look after them. They are so proud of their new class and it is a culmination of all their hard work during recruitment. They are so excited to share the joys of the sorority with them and they will feel the love from the entire house. Parents can feel secure that their daughters have an immediate family to make sure they have everything they need and are safe and secure. They will help them with their classes, getting around campus and anything else they need. If they get homesick there is always someone to talk to.

Common Misconceptions About The Greek System

The biggest misconception is that it is party, party, party all the time. In the sororities there is no alcohol allowed in the chapter houses. There are severe penalties for this, so this is a rule that is followed. Most sororities have some type of standards board. Greek women are held to a very high standard and they are told that when they go out they are a representation of that house and they must conduct themselves well. If they do not there is usually some type of sanctions imposed on them such as social probation. There is also usually a buddy system so that someone is never out at night alone or left alone at a party. There is also a House Director/Mom on the premises at all times that lives in the house. They keep a watchful eye on what goes on at the chapter house. Men are usually not allowed above the first floor without an escort and only during certain hours.

Grades suffer. This is probably the second biggest misconception. Grades are extremely important and they are accountable each quarter or semester to keep a certain GPA. If you look at a lot of Greek Systems their average GPA is higher than the university average. Houses are very competitive with each other with respect to grades, so studying is highly encouraged. You can usually find a house's average GPA on the Panhellenic website. You also have a lot of built in academic help with the upperclassmen, if needed.

All the women in the Greek System are the same. This is not the case at all. Just as many of the houses are very different and diverse each house has very different women from different backgrounds and socio-economic backgrounds. If diversity is very important to you, then this is something that is important to ask about and look for as you go through recruitment.

Conclusion

In conclusion, choosing to enter the Greek Community can be one of the best decisions you will make in your life. Like anything, it is what you make it. For me and my daughters it was a wonderful experience and we have all made very close and dear friends that we consider to be more like family. Just as every person going through is as different as every house on the campus; there is a place for anyone who truly wants to be a part of the Greek System. Although, the recruitment process may seem harsh and flawed to some, in a strange way it does usually end up working out well. That being said while you are going through the process and you realize that Greek Life is definitely not something you are interested in, that is your decision as well. You will hear about girls that go through that do not get invited to join a house. Usually this means that she many not have gotten invited to her top choices and she decides not to join. Usually what happens in this situation is that people get very shy and quiet and don't say much. Relating back to a job interview, if you were to sit in the interview and not say anything to sell yourself chances are you will not get the job. Hopefully what is outlined in this guide will help you to prepare to avoid this situation. If you take the time to prepare for recruitment it will definitely help. Try to put your best self forward and give it everything you have and you should have a very positive, albeit emotionally exhausting experience. In the end it will all be worth it.

Made in United States
Orlando, FL
18 June 2023

34275053R00029